Artistic Cats

Published by Sterling Publishing Co., Inc.
387 Park Avenue South, New York, NY 10016

Text and illustrations copyright © 2005 by Heather Hacking
Design by Janette Revill

ISBN 1-4027-3633-9

Library of Congress Cataloging-in-Publication Data Available

For information about custom editions, special sales, premium and
corporate purchases, please contact Sterling Special Sales
Department at 800-805-5489 or specialsales@sterlingpub.com.

Artistic Cats

Heather Hacking

Sterling Publishing
New York

A fragment of fresco from Thebes.

UNKNOWN OF THEBES

THE INSPIRED ARTISTS of Ancient Egypt did not leave a signature on their work. Unknown is depicted here by his brother, Also-Unknown, working on a golden sphinx, to whom there is also no answer. Unknown's assistant, A-Nony-Mouse, is painting a fresco of birds who may, or may not, have been the artist's supper.

Not seen in Ancient Egypt.

PHIDIAS

ATHENA
RULES
O.K.

$\mathcal{P}$HIDIAS IS BELIEVED to be the Greek sculptor responsible for the wonderful, ryhthmically composed marble frieze of the Parthenon. He was also known affectionately as "Fluffiarse." The frieze depicts young tomcats going clubbing on a Saturday night in fourth-century BC downtown Athens. The illustration opposite shows the master and his apprentices hard at work in the glaring heat of a Greek Friday afternoon, with their eye on the clock.

"Fluffiarse" and the boys celebrate the completion of the Parthenon.

*The School of Fluffiarse anticipating a nice
plate of mouse-aka.*

BROTHER FELIX
(Known as the Master of the Leaping Mouse)

 ONKS OF THE
Dark Ages laboriously
copied ancient, dull, lengthy
manuscripts. As a little
treat, they were allowed
to let themselves go wild
on an occasional capital let-
ter. Here Brother Felix, of
the enclosed Order of St
Tibbult-without-the-
Catflap, shows considerable
flair for color, illumination
and self-promotion.

The growing of poppies
in monastery gardens
brought a sense of
peace and calm.

"'F' for vescent!" exclaimed the exuberant Felix who
could draw but not spell.

Fra's angels start messing about.

FRA ANGELICO

*I*T SEEMS THAT someone fell asleep while filling out Fra's birth certificate. "I could have been as famous as St Francis of Assisi if I'd had a proper name," he opined devoutly. To take his mind off it, his priory gave him the task of decorating the monks' cells with angels. "I could have been Francis I of France, Francis Drake perhaps … maybe Francis Bacon, …" he muttered as he worked.

Fra Angelico looks wistfully at the famous and popular St Francis of Assisi.

SANDRO FLUFFIBOTTI

$\mathcal{T}$HE DARLING OF the Renaissance was famous for creating gorgeous "gals" such as the "Three Graces" in his *Primavera* … and the lovely goddess, borne ashore on a scallop shell in *The Birth of Venus*. Unluckily for Fluffi, there was a dearth of suitable models in Florence, and those who were vaguely palatable were often worn out by the exceptionally captivating Florentine nightlife.

Model Agency? I'm *not* happy.

Fluffibotti auditions the models for the Three Graces for his painting Primavera.

Fluffibotti finds his "Venus" asleep on the job.

*Mewcel Duchamp places the first "ready-made,"
a signed litter tray, before* Moaner Lisa.

LEO DA VINCI

*L*EO IS MOST famous for bringing a hint of a smile to his notoriously po-faced model, Moaner Lisa. He was less than amused himself when lovable Surrealist prankster Mewcel Duchamp modified the portrait with his felt-tipped pen. Da Vinci was also a prolific inventor who was courted by the crowned heads of Europe. He designed helicopters, tanks, anti-bulldog catapults and meat-seeking missiles. He was a *pip* off inventing "Concorde" when he expired in the arms of the king of France.

The Duke of Milan and the French king fight for Leo's inventions.

RAFFURAEL

THIS PAINTING BY the precociously talented Raffurael shows what fun a fishing expedition off the coast of Italy could be circa 1500. The hefty nymph Galatea is making a hen party of it when they are joined by a gang of lads whose assortment of fish-tails and hooves casts a disturbing light on the details of their family tree.

Rafurreal gets caught up in a nymphs' night out.

Happy Hour: a round of Bacardi Breezers for just six squid.

Mike gives a client some interior design advice he can't refuse.

MIKE L. ANGELO

MIKE LIVES IN Brooklyn but his family are from Florence. He does walls and ceilings mostly – and if he's doing your ceiling, you don't argue. If Mike decides you're having the *Seventh Circle of Hell* in your bathroom or Delphic sybils mooning about in your foyer, well, just go with it.

Mike L. Angelo's David's cats let him know that it is supper time.

SIR PETER PAW RUBENS

*R*UBENS PAINTED A great many large ladies. Slender cats did not take his fancy; he thought them as appealing as a praying mantis on a bed of grapefruit. This painting is his *Three Graces* and they are dancing in a circle: the resulting reverberations, if the chaos theory is correct, probably started an earthquake in Rio de Janeiro.

Rubens liked big women.

Rubens dangling dangerously over Chastity's whiskers.

Van Dyck's apprentices give the Stuart brothers a makeover.

SIR ANTHONY VAN DYCK

*V*AN DYCK SPECIALISED in dramatic paintings known as "swagger portraits." These made the rich and famous look breathtakingly gorgeous. Like Vincent van Fluff, Sir Anthony realised that a successful painter needs a van – in this instance to be able to race from stately home to royal palace. In the van were his paints, acres of lace, taffeta, silks, spare spurs, stick-on beauty spots, hat feathers, saucy garters, safety pins, knicker elastic, whisker-curling tongs and anything else it took to make a lumpy lord or drippy duke look like a celebrity.

Sir Anthony in his van.

INIGO JONES

*O*RIGINALLY A SCENERY-painter, Gary Jones soon earned the soubriquet "Inigo" for his designs for the classically inspired catflap for stately homes. Royalty and aristocrats clamoured for catflaps that had class and just a hint of Corinthian capital. The "Palladio" had an interesting octagon feature while the "Michelangelo" had a built-in paw-wiper and mudscraper.

The "Parthenon" litter tray designed by Inigo.

Inigo looks on as a royal paw returns after being out on the royal razzle.

A flurry of fur and claw envelopes the royal entourage.

DIEGO VELASWHISKERS

*T*HIS ELEGANT ARTIST was the painter to the Madrid court at a time when the Spanish royalty were going through a lingering phase of long faces, Habsburg lips and "out-to-lunch" eyes. In addition, the regal whiskers had been the victim of the Spanish Inquisition's crimping tongs … and the ladies wore skirts within which it would have been possible to hide a coach and four. Velaswhiskers had to provide flattering portraits of this raw material. Here he is attempting a likeness of the Infanta and her restless maids-in-waiting.

A Spanish royal garden party (indoors when wet).

FURMEER OF DELFT

CATS DO NOT like water and a town such as Delft, built on several canals, will inevitably contain a deeply grumpy feline population. The painter Furmeer was no exception. He cheered himself up with a delightful portrait of the maid wearing his generous little gift to her – a pilchard earring.

Mrs Furmeer discovers that her husband has been pinning pilchards on the maid.

The Girl with the Pilchard
Earring *by Furmeer.*

An aristocratic picnic:
sweet and sour partridge.

THOMAS GAINSFUR

/'HE CELEBRITY PORTRAIT painter of his day, Thomas could make his clients look wealthy and interesting, usually by incorporating a few thousand of their rolling acres in the background. This portrait of a couple who manage to look dim *and* dour at the same time is offset by the hint that they own Suffolk. Occasionally Gainsfur strayed into bohemian territory and made portraits of more lively characters such as the fiery actress Miss Hiss-Siddons.

No! My contract says <u>no</u> water!

Miss Hiss-Siddons as Ophelia.

FRANS-HISSCO GOYA

*I*T WAS PROBABLY a bad mistake from the start to have the irascible Goya paint the portrait of the permanently ratty "Iron" Duke of Wellington. Goya complained that Wellington's whiskers kept moving about; the duke declared that the picture made him look like "a gormless git;" and Goya rejoined with the Spanish for "So? Exact likeness." This historic sitting was delayed by sundry spats and hissy fits.

Goya wins on points.

Goya takes a break from painting to throttle his subject.

Blake's Ancient of Days has the "which way up?" problem with his compasses.

WILLIAM BLAKE

*A*S MAD AS a conference of hatters in Lunéville, Blake was, however, multi-talented. He could write poetry or prose, paint, engrave or draw. His pictures usually depicted mystical, ancient cats in flowing robes and white fur: he might be credited with inventing "Gandalf" long before Tolkitten. His poem *Jerusalem* has become universally famous set to music and sung as a battle hymn:

"And did those paws
In ancient time
Walk upon bedspreads nice
*   and clean?"*

It has remained a mystery how
Blake invented his strange creatures.

JOSEPH MALLARD WILLIAM TURNER

*A*N IMPRESSIONIST BEFORE his time and a feisty fighter, the duck-fancier Turner combined his pugilistic nature with an ability to "catch a moment." This painting, *Rain, Steam and Spud*, captures a terrific cat fight he had in The Dog and Duck in East London with One-Eye Billy McMullet, the Irish Heavyweight Potato-Hurler, following a disagreement over a greyhound race. Art experts point to the presence of a hare in this picture as indicating the dispute at the dog-track.

At home, Turner sketches
A Storm in a Teacup.

The atmospheric watercolor Turner
dashed off during the fight in the East End.

The terminally gloomy
Pusserpine surveys her lost lunch.

DANTE GABRIEL PUSSETTI

$\mathcal{M}$ELODRAMATIC AND MELANCHOLY to his claw-tips, painter and poet DG was a member of the Pre-Furry-ites, dedicated to creating highly emotional works in the Gothic style and often featuring knights doing dangerous things with dragons. Pussetti himself mostly depicted over-wrought "ladies," using his wife, a Curly Longhair called Frizzy, as a model. Here, however, is the ton of wavy fur and over-ripe upper lip known as Janey Morr-hiss as "Pusserpine," Queen of the Underground.

A Pre-furry-ite knight takes a lunch break.

KATSUSHIKA HOKUSAI

*H*ERE IS HOKUSAI with his poster of his finest invention: the Great Wave machine at the Kyoto fun-park. It was very innovative of him to persuade normally water-hating cats to ride the huge wave, but there was also the very popular sushi-flavoured candyfloss and tearooms where customers could spend five hours pouring a cup of tea.

The Emperor rewards Hokusai with koi carp.

Oh, dear...

SUSHI RECIPES

Surf City: the Kyoto Tourist Board's poster.

A <u>P</u>est Control Officer
at the Folies Bergère *by Manet*.

EDOUARD MANET

$\mathcal{T}$HE ELEGANT, AFFABLE Manet was a dandy and a *boulevardier*: perfectly groomed and flea-free, he mingled in café society, luxuriating in bowls of Normandy cream at the *Folies Bergère* without spilling a drop on his well-groomed whiskers. This late work shows him (in the mirror) winking and about to order a Kipper Flip and a line of catnip.

Manet the Dandy strolls along the boulevard.

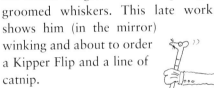

EDGAR (DOGG-ED) DEGAS

*E*D WAS AFFECTIONATELY known as "Dogg-Ed" because he stuck to his dangerous subject matter despite repeated difficulty. He painted racehorses from all angles, incurring many a kick in the whiskers. He took to pastels of "ladies of the night" at their *toilette*, which earned him several black eyes from flea-combs flung at him. He thought he would be safe in the satin shoe and tulle-tutu world of ballet: he hadn't reckoned with two dozen sets of toes in neat formation catching him under the chin in *Swan Lake*.

"Dogg-Ed" Degas discovers the dangers of drawing a lady at her toilette.

Degas bowled over by swooning swans.

Mummy catches Whisker sneaking off to "The Folies."

JAMES McNEILL WHISKER

WHISKER IS BEST remembered for his portrait of his mummy: *Whisker's Mother* or *A Portrait in Gray and Black with a Hint of Tortoiseshell*. He really wanted to paint "Girls at the Folies Bergère" and "Whooping it up at the Moulin Rouge" but his mother wouldn't let him out after 9.00 p.m. His subsequent works were rather moody.

Whisker sees his fellow artists set off for an evening on the town.

BERTHE MORISOT

"BERT," AS SHE was known by the Impressionist group, wanted to be feisty and tomcatty but Parisian manners dictated that ladies painted flowers and kittens. Her artistic skill, lively spirit and dreamy eyes inspired her friend Manet to paint her portrait many times and include a playful hint of her subversive nature. Here on *The Balcony* she sees how many *gendarmes* she can hit.

Bert is the only girl on the Impressionists' team.

*"Bert" admires her portrait
by Manet.*

Georges deciding whether whisker-tips or claw-tips deliver the better dot.

GEORGES SEURAT
(previously SEWER-RAT)

*U*NDERSTANDABLY, GEORGES CHANGED the family name when he became a celebrity. He is the artist who invented *pointillism* or "painting by dots." In this picture, *Dimanche dans le Parc de la Grande Jatte* (Sunday in the Park with a Big Cat), he captures the Parisian weekend leisure pursuit of finding discarded pet goldfish in the Seine.

Georges Seurat discovers the snags of painting by claw-tip.

PAUL CÉZANNE

$\mathcal{H}$IS SURNAME'S FIRST syllable is pronounced as one long, slow hiss, which sums up Cézanne's life and general demeanor. As in this portrait by Cat Pissarro, he was a picture of disgruntled grumpiness. He was also a legendary miser, which explains why he painted the same view of Mont St Victoire thirty-two times – he was too cheap to pay the bus fare to another location. He is considered to be the leading post-Impressionist because he could paint a reasonable impression of a post.

Cézanne gets around more after he receives his bus pass.

Paul Cézanne, *by Pissarro, cheerfully displaying
views of* that *mountain.*

*Gauguin stumbles upon
a mango-throwing contest in Tahiti.*

PAUL GAUGUIN

AUGUIN WAS ONE of those restless types who gets on people's nerves after a while. He certainly unsettled fellow artist and flatmate Vincent van Fluff, to the extent that Vincent's paw shook a lot while shaving. Having annoyed most of Paris and Brittany, Go-Gauguin (as he was called) took himself off to Tahiti to paint Polynesian cats lounging under palm trees. He thought this was primitive and interesting and would make him a bundle. Wrong on three counts.

Vincent has had enough of Gauguin's bad temper.

JOHN "SWINGER" SARGENT

$\mathcal{S}$IMILARLY TO VAN DYKE, Sargent was an exponent of the "swagger" portrait which flattered and improved the upper crust. He prowled about on the high-society fence-tops of London, Paris, Florence and New York, carousing and caterwauling with great panache. Here is his sassy painting of Lady Sassoon in superb swagger mode.

Sargent at a fence-top cocktail party in "swinging" society.

All the feathers and the fine hand-held carp were caught personally by Her Ladyship.

La Goulue and her goldfish entertain at
La Moulin de la Galette.

HENRI TOOTH-
LESS LAUTREC

*T*HIS ARISTOCRATIC TORTOISESHELL was very small but exquisitely marked. He was so *petit* that he could shelter under dachsunds on rainy nights. He was also quiet and discreet – possibly because his *louche* lifestyle had caused his teeth to fall out. He loved to prowl the Parisian boulevards after dark from dodgy brasserie to seedy café, tippling absinthe and cream. Or he would stroll to the dance halls, where, perched on a very high bar stool, he could sketch the can-can dancers. This poster shows a strapping ginger lass nicknamed "La Goulue" (fond of food).

Henri Toothless Lautrec joins the can-can girls at the Mewlin Rouge.

HENRI MAT-HISS

$\mathcal{M}$AT-HISS WAS a member of the artistic group known as the Fauves (the Wild Beasts) because they were desperately unconventional and untamed. However, Mat-hiss went *too* far: he was *so* beastly, so hissy and spitty, rolling on the floor and biting the fringes off the mat, back legs kicking like pistons, that the Fauves threw him out. Home alone, his house mice drove him to distraction with their little pranks.

Mat-hiss and the Wild Beasts: "Deranged" Derain, the hard-up Georges Broque and Vlamink, a White Russian Polecat.

Mat-hiss's mice rearrange a composition.

The posters go up for the first night of Salami,
a play in three slices.

PAWBREY BEARDSLEY

*T*HIS SUPERBLY DECADENT illustrator shared, with Whisker Wilde, a secret passion for salami. In this portrait Pawbrey unveils his cover design for Whisker's play *Salami* dedicated to Italian sausage. The wickedly impish illustrator has drawn a caricature of the tubby playwright as the full moon. Wilde, a notorious humorist, found this mildly unfunny.

Beardsley also illustrated the life of King Arthur.

ART NOUVEAU

$\mathcal{B}$ORN ARTHUR NEWEY in *fin de siècle* Cardiff, Art moved to Paris, changed his name and became a one-cat art movement typifying the decadent and languid lifestyle of Montmartre alleys. Art's café *Le Chat Noir* attracted many artists and writers: the Czech poster-artist Alphonse Moocher; writer Whisker Wilde; artist Pawbrey Beardsley; lampshade-maker Tiffany Glass and the actress Sarah Heartburn – anyone who could roll some *Gauloise* catnip and look *louche* until the small hours was welcome.

Tiffany Glass, Whisker Wilde, Pawbrey Beardsley, Sarah Heartburn and her pet borzoi.

*Art encouraging Moocher to finish his poster
of the Divine Sarah.*

*A mouse is uncertain whether the cat in the hat
considers him cute or tasty.*

PURR-AUGUSTE RENOIR

*R*ENOIR LIKED TO paint Parisians having a good time in the open air. Here, at *La Grenouillère* (the Froggery) on a rural section of the Seine, he is painting *The Luncheon of the Mousing Party*.

There are snags to painting in the open air.

HENRI (LE DOUANIER) POUSSEAU

*I*T IS NOT often that one finds cats employed as customs officers (*douaniers)* but to come across one who also paints in the "naïve" style is almost unique. Henri liked jungle scenes because they didn't remind him of his day job. For this picture he had wanted to draw a Bengali tiger from life in an authentic setting. However, he couldn't afford to travel on Custom Service pay. He had to settle for using his neighbour, Fat Ginge, as a model, and a few potted plants from his auntie's conservatory.

Henri was nicknamed "Inspector Pousseau" in his job at Customs.

Henri arranges Ginge for a sitting.

Monet planning lunch.

CLAWED MONET

MONET DESIGNED A water feature for himself in his garden at Giverny and specialised thereafter in painting only aquatic plants. He wanted to be known as "The One that Paints Water-Lilies." This stopped people confusing him with Manet (or so he thought). A gourmet of considerable girth, Monet also hoped to lure frogs towards his paintings and then into Mme Monet's grill pan.

A winter scene by Monet.

PURRBLO PICATSSO

*L*IKE MIRÓ AND Dali, Picatsso was a Spanish artist with a colorful character. He had himself marinated in neat, distilled essence of a Parisian smoke-filled café and went from *kitten terrible* to feisty old tomcat and through more artistic phases than most cats have fish dinners. This picture shows the wily old fox surrounded by just some of his art trends: the Blue Persian ladies, Cubist ladies, the hefty ladies, ladies with African masks ... so at least *one* theme remained constant in his ever-changing repertoire.

Picatsso often paid his restaurant bill with a little drawing.

*Purrblo changed his style more often than
most artists changed their underpants.*

Munch binge-munching herring "Munchies."

EDVARD MUNCH

$\mathcal{T}$HIS NORWEGIAN ARTIST, frequently depressed, had two great claims to fame: he painted *The Scream* and invented "Munchies" (original herring flavor). No-one quite knows what Munch was symbolising in this picture but art critics suspect that it is the pain and chagrin of the cat-owner repeatedly woken at 4.00 a.m. by cats rocketing around the bedroom.

waaaah!!

Edvard out with the Munch children.

FURIDA
KAHLO

$\mathcal{T}$HE MEXICAN ARTIST Furida Kahlo staggered the art world by being able to paint and be a female. This was unusual in art history. Her paintings always showed a depiction of herself sporting her signature mono-brow, a feature of her unusual tortoiseshell marking and a symbol of her fiesty nature which she maintained on a diet of cactus *tortillas*.

Cactus Tortillas

Cactus, Spinefish and Sea Urchin Soup

Cactus mousse

Tequila Toothpicks

Furida plans a dinner party.

Furida paints the prettiest cat she knows.

SYLVESTER DALI

*M*OST ARTISTS ARE as mad as a sackful of squid, but Dali takes the prize. Apart from his surreal paintings, he produced many strange "objects" to accompany his weird lifestyle. Here is Himself, as an installation, taking a call on his lobster phone, wearing his kipper tie, herringbone jacket and sprats.

By contrast, there was the strait-laced work of Dali's contemporary, Pet Mondrian.

Take one Mondrian before bedtime.

Dali: dream or nightmare?

Marked and the missus on a trip.

MARKED CHAGALL

*T*HIS PRETTILY PATTERNED Russian painted pictures which mostly illustrated his own life so that he could show off his unusual coloring. To add to this, he placed himself and his lovely bride in some unusual settings – such as flying through the air and jumping over the moon. This has led to speculation that his home life included something a little "consciousness-enhancing" in the bed-time milk.

Chagall's friends found his bridal fantasies rather schmaltzy.

JACKSON THE UNPOLLOCKED

*T*HIS NEUTERED TOM had to find *some* substitute for carousing. He took up painting but failed to make an impact and so turned to frantic binge-eating, knocking over pans and cans of sauces and jams in his bid to reach food. The resulting mess on the kitchen floor was spotted by an art critic, adored … and installed as modern art – and the fame of "Jack the Dripper" was born. What a happy accident.

Mrs Unpollocked regretted letting Jackson wind her knitting wool.

*Jackson observes the baked bean of eternity falling on
the floor of perpetual doom.*

Rothko modifies a painting in a Marked manner.

MARKED ROTHKO

$\mathcal{T}$'HIS TEMPERAMENTAL TORTOISESHELL took pique to the heights of honed perfection. Perpetually outraged, he earned the nickname "Wrath-of-God-ko." To calm himself, he borrowed some rollers and hundreds of gallons of Army surplus paint, and created huge canvases of moody nothingness. These took New York's art critics' fancy and Rothko would have been a huge commercial success had his legendary temper and unclipped claws not got in the way.

"Wrath-of-God-Ko" attacks a canvas.

FRANCE-HISS BACON

*H*ERE IS THE epitome of the tortured and tetchy artist. Frequently high as a kite on catnip liqueur, Bacon was often to be found caterwauling past midnight in a Soho alley where, annoyingly, graffiti called him a "ham" artist. His irritation is reflected in his work: he painted truly horrific portraits of subjects yowling, howling, hissing and biting; it was hard to tell which was the painting and which was the artist.

France-hiss's mother suggests he paints Singing Nuns instead of Screaming Popes.

Life imitates art: Bacon and his Spitting Pope.

Bandy has a wobble on the wild side.

BANDY WARHOL

*B*ANDY WAS THE wispy, white-haired wonder with a funny walk. He hung about with various strange strays in New York alleys, getting high as a kite and rolling about in catnip. The resulting blurred vision produced his famous multiple portrait of Marilyn Codroe and an enigmatic silkscreen image of a can of Whiskas.

Bandy and other members of "The Velvet Underpants" at a New York catnip party.

89

DAMIEN HIRSUTE

CHUNKY AND STUBBLY-furred, Damien was watching his granny's goldfish one day when he had his divine inspiration for an installation: a half-minnow in formaldehyde. He would have liked a shark for more impact but size, cost and availability prohibited it. So he nipped to his local fishmonger and had him slice the minnow neatly and place it in the tank. Art entrepreneur Charles Scraatchi was impressed and exhibited it in his famous Scraatchi Gallery. The art world flipped. Damien was able to move out of his gran's flat and into a forty-turreted castle with pool. His *Half-Clam in Aspic* is permanently on show at the Tat Modern, London.

Damien Hirsute's taxidermist stuffs a tadpole.

Frying tonight! Damien and fans at a "private view."

Tracey scrutinises the workmanship on her Stuffed Sparrow.

TRACEY EMIN-ENTLY FAMOUS

*T*HIS LONG-FACED Maltese Cross can be a mite crotchety at times. However, she is famous for producing some astounding work. Her *Unmade Cat-Basket* was purchased by Charles Scraatchi and really looks amazingly like an unmade cat-basket. She has also exhibited a beach hut, a stuffed sparrow and a quilt. This is the sort of thrilling stuff that can fill up an art gallery in no time. An "A-list" celebrity, Tracey is often seen at openings: envelopes, pop-studs, zips, an eye, pantry doors, catflaps – anywhere and everywhere.

Celebrities celebrate the opening of a Soho catflap.

JACK VETERINARIAN

*J*ACK'S HAUNTING BEACH scenes have proved universally popular as paintings, prints and greetings cards. It is less well-known that before becoming a painter, Jack was a Scottish vet specialising in tropical diseases. Unfortunately this will remain a somewhat limited career in Scotland until global warming really gets going – so Jack began a successful career in painting. He is, however, willing to suggest a cure when an art critic has a bad case of apoplexy.

The Sunday Clarion

BUT IS IT ART?

VET on CALL

Jack carefully bandages an injured art critic.

"Jack the Vet" and his best-known painting: The Purring Butler.